Spiritual Letters of Fénelon

Spiritual Letters

of

Francois De Salignac De La Mothe-Fénelon

IDLEWILD PRESS
Cornwall-on-Hudson, N. Y.

Printed in the United States of America
by The Cornwall Press

Translator's Note

So far as I have been able to find out, all editions
of the works of Fénelon are long since out of print.
Moreover, the only editions which I have come
across in either French or English since the original
French edition of 1858 have been excerpts. Excerpts
in French with the imprimatur of a Roman Catholic
Bishop with Quietism left out, excerpts in English
by a Boston Unitarian with Catholicism left out and
more recently excerpts by an Anglican with the at-
mosphere of Versailles left out. This does not seem
to me fair treatment of one of the great lights of
French literature and of world Christianity.

In this small book, I have translated two groups of
the letters of Fénelon from the old 1858 edition,
forty letters to the Countess of Gramont, (Letters
202-241, Volume 2) and eight letters to a soldier
(Letters 41-48, Volume 2). These two groups were
written during the same period, and seem to contain
the essence of Fénelon's teaching. Both groups were
written to people in the world, and are surprisingly
relevant to the lay reader today. I have omitted noth-

ing in the original text except one or two formal end-
ings.

I wish to express my thanks to the Rev. Charles F.
Whiston for his help and encouragement and for
introducing me to Fénelon, to Mrs. Lenore Turn-
bull for procuring for me the complete five volumes
of Fénelon's works, and to Mrs. Jessie Hassler for
many hours of typing.

MILDRED WHITNEY STILLMAN.

Cornwall-on-Hudson, N.Y.
September, 1945.

Foreword

Over many years now I have observed how person after person, to whom I have loaned my own copies of the Spiritual Letters of Fénelon, have been powerfully blessed from such reading. Believing that many more would also find rich spiritual guidance and help, were the Letters again made available in English, I have urged Mrs. Stillman to use her ready knowledge of French to give to us the Spiritual Letters in English translation, of which this little book is a first selection.

These letters were written by a great archbishop in France toward the close of the 17th Century, but they deal with those fundamental matters of the soul, which are the same in every age. They were written by one who was a Master in the spiritual life, one who knew God deeply and truly, who knew the spiritual needs of men accurately, and who knew well the ways of God's workings upon the lives of men and women. The Letters require and deserve many, repeated readings, if their deep and rich meanings are to be grasped. They should therefore be read slowly, prayerfully, humbly. Through much faithful rereading of the Letters God will offer you a rich spiritual companionship with Himself, and with one of His greatest servants—Fénelon.

Charles F. Whiston.

Church Divinity School of the Pacific,
Berkeley, California.

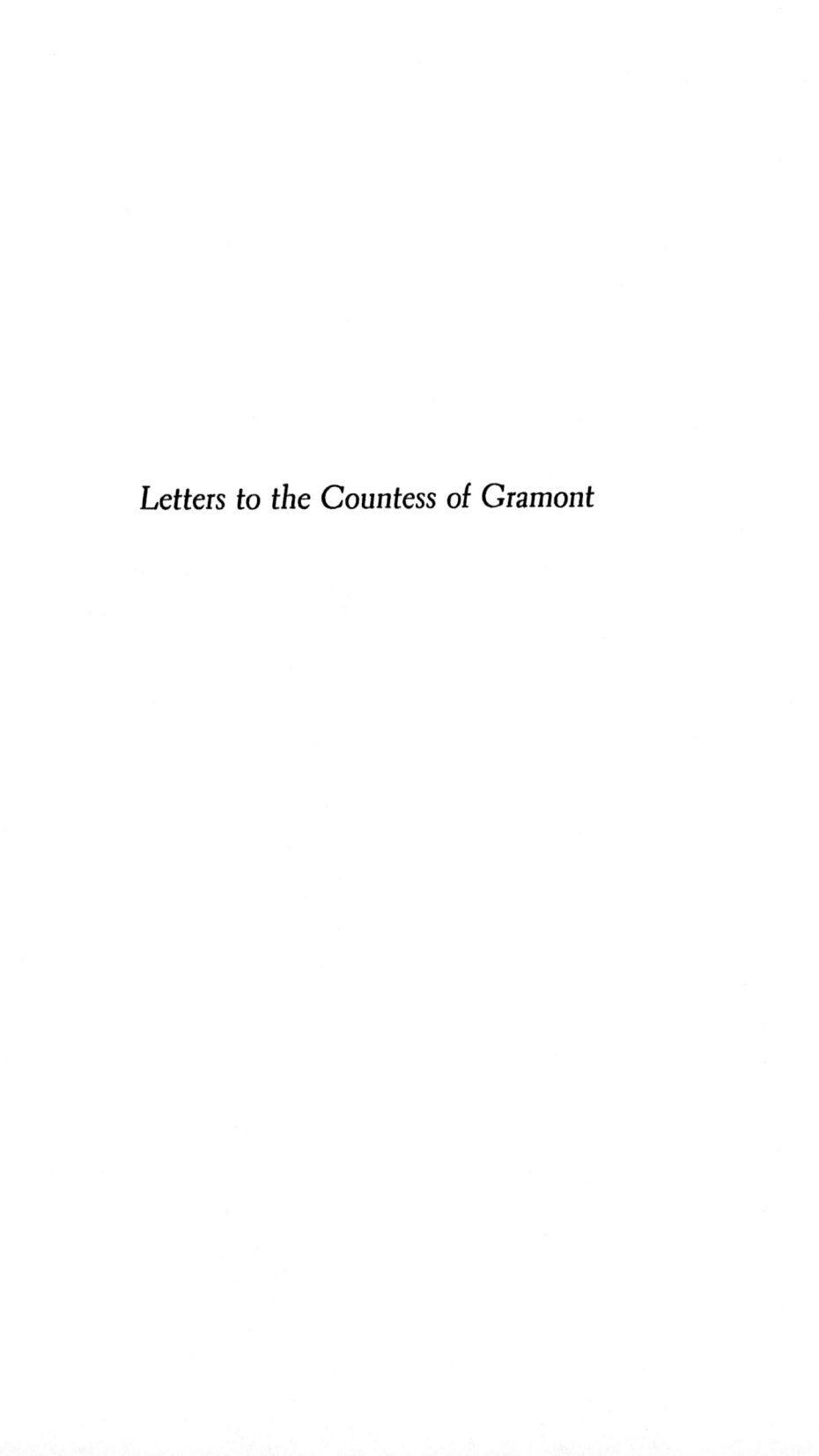

Letters to the Countess of Gramont

Elizabeth Hamilton, Countess of Gramont, to whom the following letters are addressed, was born in 1641, the daughter of George, Count Hamilton of Scotland, and of Marie Butler. She married, about 1660, Philibert de Gramont, son of Antoine de Gramont, second of the name, and known by the memoirs published under his name.

After her marriage, the Countess soon became lady in waiting to the Queen, Marie-Therese of Austria, wife of Louis XIV. We can imagine how hard it must have been for this young Scotch girl to accustom herself to life at Versailles. She wished to give herself wholly to God, and about 1684, put herself under the guidance of Abbé Fénelon. Without being her confessor, he was her spiritual director until his banishment from court in 1697.

I

I was in the country, madame, when you did me
the honor of writing me a note dated from your retreat. If I had been in Paris I should not have missed
going there to receive your commands. I hope that
some trip which you will make here, or some matter
which will take me to Versailles will make up to me
for what I have missed. You may be sure of one
thing, madame, that I wish you always, from the
depths of my heart, the self-control and the fidelity
to the mind of God, which you need to overcome the
dangers of your position. You have much to fear,
both within and without. Without the world smiles
on you, and that part of the world most capable of
swelling pride, gives yours food for flattery, by the
marks of consideraion which you receive at court.
Within, you have to overcome a taste for luxury, a
haughty and scornful spirit, and frivolous habits of
long standing. All this put together is like a torrent
which carries you away, despite the best resolutions.
The true remedy for so much which is bad, is to save,
before everything else, some regular time for prayer

and for reading. You know, madame, what I have had the honor of saying to you many times on this subject, I pray our God that he take you away from all, rather than to leave you in the clutches of the world.

II

Tues. Dec. 10, 1686

I know, madame, that the scandal which has just broken out has upset you as such things have before. I truly feel for you, and am interested in everything which affects you. What makes me most indignant in these unfortunate affairs, is that the world, which is only too accustomed to judge ill of the good, concludes that there are none such upon earth. Some are delighted to believe this, and triumph in it maliciously; others are troubled, and despite a certain desire which they have to turn towards the good, they remain kept away from devotion by their distrust of all the devout. People are astonished to see one who gave the impression of being a good man or, to be more exact, one who really was converted in solitude, fallen again in his desires and habits, when exposed to the world. Do they not know that men are weak, that worldliness is catching, that weak people can only save themselves by avoiding a wrong environment? Then what is there new about this? A lot of noise over the crash of a tree which had no roots and was attacked by every wind! After all hasn't the world its hypocrites in business as well as in religion? Should the men of pretended honesty make us be-

lieve there are no true ones? When people make a
lot of such a scandal, they show that they do not
really know either man or virtue. We ought to be
saddened by such a scandal, but we should be surprised at nothing, when we understand the depths of
human misery, and to what extent the little good
which we do accomplish is within us like something
loaned. Let him who is upright tremble lest he fall.
Let him who is on the ground, grovelling in the mire,
not triumph over the fall of one of those who had
appeared upstanding. Our trust is neither in weak
men, nor in ourselves, as weak as all the rest. It is in
God alone, who is immutable truth. Let all men
show that they are only men, that is to say worthless, lies and sin; let them allow themselves to be carried away by the flood of iniquity; the truth of God
will not be at all weakened by that, and the world
will only be the more abominable, for having corrupted those who sought for virtue.

As for the hypocrites, time unmasks them and they
always betray themselves in some way. They are only
hypocrites to enjoy the fruits of their hypocrisy.
Either their life is soft and amusing, or their behavior
is self-interested and ambitious. We watch them
scheme, flatter, take on different personalities. A
truly good person is simple, integrated, unforced,
open. He neither pushes nor abases himself. He is

neither jealous of reputation nor of success. He does the least harm which he can. He lets himself be judged and is silent. He is content with little. He has no cabal, no design, no pretention. Hypocrisy may imitate all this, but very crudely. When we are deceived, it is from lack of attention, or lack of experience of true goodness. People who are not at all familiar with diamonds, or who do not look at them closely enough, can take an imitation for a fine gem; but it is none the less true that there are real diamonds, and that it is not impossible to recognize them. The truth is that in order to trust ourselves to people who seem good, we must have recognized in them a conduct, simple, solid, constant and tested, avoiding all affectation, but firm and vigorous in the things which are essential.

III

Sunday, June 12, 1689

My health is good, thanks to God, madame. It is in a condition to justify quinquina,* and to silence all its enemies. Your kind thoughtfulness gives me deep pleasure, and I am glad of my fever for having brought it to me. Your discretions, madame, are absurd. When you wish me to have the honor of seeing, you have only to give me your orders. Simple and natural behavior is too pleasing to God, to shock those who wish to serve him, and who should in his name recommend simplicity. So be simple in all things, madame, and simple in sending for me, as in all the rest. I hope that you can straighten out the troublesome matters which bring you to Paris. I imagine that you will see a very giddy person, because the trip will have turned her head. There are very different ways of being intoxicated. Scripture says: Woe unto you who are drunk, and not from wine! There are intoxications from pride, others from anger and from vengeance; there are others from zeal and ardor. It is thus that the apostles appeared drunken, when they received the Holy Spirit. On your return,

* quinquina—cinchona bark from which quinine is made.

madame, I hope to find you in this kind of inebria-
tion. In the meanwhile I shall pray with my whole
heart for you.

IV

Paris, Aug. 25, 1689

I am very mortified, madame, by the promptness with which you did me the honor of writing to me, and the slowness with which I send you my humble thanks, but no one knows better than you, madame, how to forgive the faults which come from embarrassment. You know what I ought to think of what has just happened to me. You, who groan at the court, you, madame, should pray God in charity for those who go there. You will never find anyone there, who will be with a more sincere respect than I am, madame, your etc.*

* The above note is in thanks for the Countesse's interest in Fénelon's nomination as tutor to the Duke of Bourgoyne, grandson of Louis XIV.

V

Sunday, Oct. 2, 1689

I think, madame, that you have two things to do, one with regard to your affairs, one with regard to yourself. The first, which concerns your activities, is to take care to save a little time from the world, for your reading and prayers. It seems to me that I visualize all your difficulties, I am bringing them to mind so forcefully; but, after all, our duties must come each in its place, and salvation must rank first. What would you say of a person who would not find time to eat or sleep? Time given to the necessities of life, you would say, is the best use of time even for the sake of our activities. If your health gives out, how will you get anything done? And what good will your work do, if you do not live to reap its fruits? I tell you the same thing, madame. If you let your soul be used up, and fail from lack of nourishment, what will all your social contacts amount to, and not only these but the things which seem most important, most necessary and most pressing? *Martha, Martha, you are careful and troubled about many things!* Mary, whom you see recollected and quiet, has chosen the better part, which shall never be taken away from her.

Nevertheless, madame, I do not say all this to make you feel compunction over necessary occupations; but rest assured that the necessary occupations will never go well unless you leave time to eat your daily bread for your own nourishment; because God is too good, and has made you too sensible of his mercies, to deprive you of the means of prayer, and of sustaining yourself in the feelings with which he inspires you. Consider then, madame, saving a half hour, mornings and evenings. By pretending to wake up later in the morning, and in the evening by having some letter to write, you can get away, and your real duties will be done no less well. Also you must take advantage of every odd moment, when you are waiting for someone, when you go from one place to another, when you are with people whose talk runs on, so that all you need to do is to let them talk, you can lift your heart to God for a moment and by so doing refresh yourself in the midst of your activities. The less time one has, the more important it is to manage it. If a person waits to have regular and convenient hours by himself, in order to fill them with serious things, he runs the risk of waiting too long, especially in the kind of life which you lead; but one must take advantage of every broken moment. The life of prayer is not like the world's business. Worldly affairs need regular time freed for long consecutive application, but worship does not need such hard or such consistent application; in one moment one can recall the presence of God, love him, adore him, offer him what we are doing or what we are suffering, and in his presence calm all the agitation of our hearts. So take a half-hour in the morning madame and another half-hour in the afternoon, to repair the breaches which the world makes; and as the day goes by, make use of a few of the thoughts which mean most to you, to renew yourself in the presence of God.

The other thing which you need to do, for your own sake, is not to be at all discouraged, either by the experience of your own weakness, or by your disgust with the hectic life which you lead. It is a blessing of God that you do groan at this merry-go-round, and the groaning is the antidote which keeps your heart from being corrupted by the frivolity at court. For this reason I should feel very sorry, if that life ceased to displease you. Your complaints and your disgust give me a true joy. God will make you mortify yourself by disgust for the world, if it is sincere, in the midst of the world itself; just as he has made other people mortify themselves in solitude and by being deprived of all that the world can give. It is only a question of being faithful, patient and peaceful in the crosses of our present state, which we ourselves have not chosen, and which God has given according to his own design.

As for our faults, they are harder to bear; but they turn to our advantage, if we use them to humble ourselves, without relaxing our efforts to correct ourselves. Discouragement would not get you anywhere. It would only be the despair of a vexed self-love. The only way to profit by the humiliation of our faults, is to face them in all their ugliness, without losing hope in God, and without having any hope in ourselves. Never did a person need more urgently to be humiliated by her faults than you do. Only thus will God crush your pride and confound your intellectual conceit. When God has taken away all of your resources, he will build his own edifice. Until then, he will demolish everything by your own faults. Allow him to do this. Work humbly without counting on anything.

When you wish me to have the honor of seeing you from time to time, I will go to the house of the Duchess of Chevreuse.

VI

Thurs. Feb. 25, 1690

I am very happy to learn, madame, that you at last are finding a way to keep a few hours of solitude for yourself. To open your door very late, and act as though you have been still sleeping, besides seeking a quiet place outside of your own home, these are good ways to protect yourself from all who would disturb you. During the rest of the day, you can cut things a little short with some people, who only want to entertain you, or who want to involve you in their affairs more than they have a right to. It is a great consolation to think that God conceals himself in a person who annoys us, as he conceals himself in the noblest of your friends. We must see in the face of the intruder, God who made us all, and who is no less careful to mortify us by annoyances, than he is to teach us and touch us by good examples. The troublesome person whom Gods sends to us, serves to break our will, to upset our schedule, to make us more eager for silence and recollection, to detach us from our plans, from our rest, from our conveniences and from our tastes; to modify our own spirit in order to accommodate it to that of another; to confound us every time that impatience escapes us

in this interference, to stir in our hearts a greater
hunger for God, even while he seems to withdraw
from us because of all this bother.

Not that we should take the initiative and expose
ourselves ever by our own choice to frivolous company. God forbid! That would be to tempt God,
and to look for danger; but as for the providential
interruptions from which we try to shield ourselves
by reserving hours for reading and prayer, you may
feel sure that these will turn out all for the best.
Everything which is in the hands of God bears fruit.
Often even these very things which make you sigh
for solitude, are more useful to you by humbling you
and making you give up your own life, than the most
profound solitude would be. Let us go on as God
leads us, day by day, putting each moment to use,
without looking ahead. Sometimes a wonderful
book, a fervent meditation, or an inspiring conversation, may flatter our taste, make us feel content and
complacent, persuade us that we are well advanced,
and in giving us beautiful thoughts about our crosses,
only make us more haughty and irritable toward
those whom we find in our path, as we go forth from
all these holy exercises.

Keep then, madame, to this simple rule. Seek
nothing distracting, but bear calmly everything which
God gives you against your own wish, to upset you.

What illusion! We seek God far off in perhaps impossible projects, and we do not dream that we can possess him right here in the midst of all the turmoil of the world, in a state of pure faith, if we bear, humbly and bravely, the troublesomeness of his creatures here and our own imperfections.

I have only one thing to say to you about love of your neighbor. Only humility will soften you in that respect. Only the sight of your own wretchedness can make you sympathetic and tolerant towards that of another. You will say to me, *I can see that humility should make me bear with my neighbor, but what will give me humility?* Two things put together will produce it. Never separate them. The first is the view of the abyss of misery from which the powerful hand of God has drawn you, and over which he still holds you as though suspended in the air. The second is the presence of God, who is all. It is only in looking steadfastly at God, and in loving him, that we forget ourselves, that we free ourselves from this bauble which has dazzled us, and that we become accustomed to finding refuge in our smallness under the lofty majesty which engulfs everything. Love God, and you will be humble. Love God and you will no longer love yourself. Love God and you will love all that he wishes you to love for love of him.

VII

Tues. March 21, 1690

I do not think, madame, that you need trouble yourself at all over your confessions and your past communions. If the beginnings have been irregular, at least they have been in good faith, and you have thereby committed faults because of a virtue quite contrary to your natural character, I mean because of your simplicity. Besides you must realize that the integrity of past confessions consists, not in not having omitted any sins, but merely of accusing yourself candidly of all those which you recognized at that time. At that time you did not have sufficient light to see, in the depths, many stirrings of evil and depraved human nature which were commencing to develop. As the light increases, we find ourselves more corrupt than we thought. We are astonished at our former blindness, and we see emerge from the bottom of our hearts, as from a deep cavern, a myriad of shameful inclinations, like nasty and poisonous snakes. We should never have dreamed that we carried such things in our breasts, and we feel a horror of ourselves, as we see them emerge. We must neither be astonished nor discouraged. It is not that we are more wicked than we were. On the contrary, we are less so. But as our sins diminish, the light which shows them to us grows, and we are seized with horror. But remember, for your comfort, that we only notice our sins when we are commencing to be cured of them.

When a person has lost all source of healing, he does not feel in the least the depth of his misery. He is in the state of blindness, conceit and hardness where he is left entirely to himself. In letting himself go with the stream, a person does not feel its swiftness; but the current makes itself felt, to the degree more or less with which the swimmer struggles against it. If you see definite and important things which you have omitted in your first confessions, tell them simply the first time that you go again to confession. Your confessor is upright, discreet and godly. As for everything else, go your way in peace. Remember that humility, frequent silence and recollection will do you more good than all the austerities and all the pains by which you would like to do penance. Above all for you silence is the most important. Even when you can not get away from people, you will often be able to keep still, and let others do the talking. You can only control your scornful, mocking and haughty spirit, by keeping it on the leash of silence. Keep a stern watch over your lips. The presence of God, which will restrain your words, will also guard your every thought and your every desire. This work will be accomplished little by little. Have patience with yourself as with others.

VIII

I think, madame, that you should now cultivate the habit of silence, so far as good breeding in conversation will permit. Silence keeps us more easily in the presence of God, avoids for us many rude and supercilious remarks, in short, suppresses a great number of sallies or criticisms which may hurt our neighbors. Silence humbles the spirit and detaches it little by little from the world. It makes a kind of solitude in our hearts, like that which you would wish for. It will supply all that you lack in the difficulties in which you find yourself. If you do not talk needlessly you will have plenty of free moments even in the midst of people whom you are with against your own wishes.

You would like to have freedom to pray to God, and God, who knows better than you do what you need, gives you difficulties and restraints to discipline you. The discipline which comes by the will of God will do you more good than would the sweetness of prayer, which would be your own choice and your own taste.

You know very well, madame, that times for retreat are not necessary in order to love God. When he gives you the time, you must take it and profit by it. Until then, live in a state of faith, believing that whatever he gives you is for the best. Lift up your heart often to him, without noticing anything external. Only talk when it is necessary. Bear patiently whoever interrupts you. As you understand religion, God treats you according to your need. You need to be humbled more than you do to receive illumination. The one thing which I fear for you in this state is distraction, but you can avoid this by silence.

If you are faithful in keeping silent, when it is not necessary to speak, God will give you the grace to remain recollected, when you talk because you have to. When you are not free to save long periods of time, be careful to manage brief ones. Fifteen minutes, kept by careful managing and faithfulness under difficulties, will be worth as much to God as the whole hours which you would give him in a more free time. Besides, different odd moments taken throughout the day, will add up to quite a considerable amount. Perhaps this way will even be an advantage because you will turn to God more frequently than if you were only giving him one regular time.

To love, to remain silent, to endure, to act against your wishes, so that you can do God's will by adapting your own to that of your neighbor, this, madame, is your part. How fortunate you are, to carry the cross which God gives you with his own hands in the working out of his providence! The penances which we choose, or which we accept when they are given us, do not begin to do away with our self-love, as do those which God hands to us himself every day. These have nothing upon which our own will can rely, and as they come directly from a merciful providence, they bring with them a grace proportional to our needs. We have only to surrender ourselves daily to God, without looking ahead. He will carry us in his arms, as a tender mother carries her child. Let us believe, hope, love with all the simplicity of children. In our every need, let us turn our eyes fondly and confidently toward our heavenly Father. Remember what he says in Holy Scripture: *Though even a mother should forget her own son, the fruit of her womb, I would forget you never.*

IX

Versailles, May 28,
before 1695

You are afraid, madame, of being unfaithful to
God in your duties, and you are right. Nothing so
blocks grace as a sluggish soul, which by wanting
freedom, refuses to God what it feels he demands,
or else delays. However, we must also avoid falling
into over-scrupulousness. Consider simply, then, on
every occasion, what true courtesy demands. Sup-
pose, for instance, just as you are going to say your
prayers and do your reading, someone arrives unexpectedly from outside, who never comes at that time,
who has real business with you, one whom you do
not know well enough to ask to come back later, and
who would be rightly offended if you did. It stands
to reason, madame, that you ought to leave your de-
votional exercises to fulfill this obligation, but in that
case, you must try to make up at some other time
during the day, what you have lost at the time of the
interruption, just as we dine at two o'clock, when
company arriving unexpectedly has prevented us
from dining at noon. As for the people who have
no real business to attend to, and whom you could
see later, or those who only come to pass the time,

and for their own pleasure, in these situations it is only right to send the callers away. You must be strictly fair in all this. Never did a person need more than you, inner nourishment, silence, reflection, escape from the world, distrust of her self and of the desires of her own heart. You could not break off too completely from the pleasures of worldly chatter. You must put yourself down continuously. You will always bounce back too high. You must humble yourself, become a child, wrap yourself in swaddling clothes, and give yourself gruel. You will still be a naughty child. All the crosses which God is giving you, and under which he wishes to bend you, do not yet restrain your pride in the least.

It will only be when you yourself renounce your own spirit, in the silence before God, that you will be made meek and gentle by grace. Speak when you are alone. Then you will not talk too much, because it will be to God that you will speak of your troubles, your needs and your good desires. But in company, you can hardly make the mistake of talking too little. This does not have to be a dry and supercilious silence however. On the contrary, it must be a silence of deference to others. I shall be delighted to have you talk, to praise, approve, agree, defer or help; but I am sure that when you only speak in this fashion, you will speak very little, and that the conversation will seem to you dull. Limit yourself then madame, to speaking little, to speaking simply and modestly, to preferring others to yourself in every thing, and to keeping recollected even in conversation. You have a greater need than most for this antidote. You know the extent of my interest and respect.

X

Versailles, June 22

The letter which you did me the honor of writing
o me, madame, has been long on the road. I have
ust received it, judge the speed by that. I under-
tand that you are suffering, and are making others
uffer. You must work bravely and steadily to bear
our own burden and to relieve your neighbor. Every
int of distrust and of superiority, every spirit of
:riticism and of mockery shows a self-centered mind,
which is not conscious of its own wretchedness,
which gives itself up to its sensibilities, which takes
ll its pleasure in the faults of others. Nothing should
be so quick to humiliate us as this kind of pride, easy
to wound, mocking, supercilious, haughty, jealously
wishing everything for itself, and always intolerant
towards the faults of others. We are surely imperfect,
when we can not stand the imperfections of those
about us. For so much wrong I see no remedy but
hope in God, who is as good and as powerful as you
are weak and bad. Nevertheless, he will let you lan-
guish a long time, without uprooting your nature and
habits, because it is much more important for you to
be crushed by your own wretchedness, and by feeling your powerlessness to emerge from it, than it

would be to enjoy all of a sudden the pleasure of se
ing yourself made perfect! Think only of bearir
with others, of turning your eyes away from peop.
who are not good for you, as we shut our eyes again:
a temptation. Such people are a very dangerous on
for you. Pray, read, humble your spirit by a taste fc
simple things. Soften your heart by uniting it wit
the child Jesus, and be serene in your humiliatior
Seek your strength in silence.

I am delighted that you are touched by Madam
Mortemart's progress. She is truly good, and want
to be more and more so. Virtue costs her quite a
much as it does another, and in that she is well fitte
to encourage you. No one is more interested than
am, madame, in the things about which you feel th
most deeply.

XI

Tues. June 27, 1690

I am, deeply touched madame by the painful state
n which you are. I think I see clearly its source. If
ou can make up your mind to use the simple remedy
vhich I am going to propose to you, you will soon be
·elieved, but I fear that some scruple may stop you
:rom doing so.

The excessive fear of enjoying pleasure in harm-
.ess and necessary things does more harm to your
;piritual advancement, than the pleasure itself could
do. It is true that we must never flatter ourselves,
especially when we need to punish ourselves, but a
perpetual struggle to get rid of even a slight involuntary feeling of pleasure in a regulated life causes you
a very harmful disquiet. I should like, therefore, to
take away the excessive fastidiousness and luxurious
tastes every time that you are aware of them, but I
by no means should want to have a strained consci-
entiousness continually give up the pleasures in-
evitably attached to simple food and necessary rest.
Since you are told to take milk to build up your
blood, you should do, so far as fasting goes, what
your doctor tells you. We must, without arguing, let
ourselves be judged, after we have made our action

clear. Otherwise we perplex ourselves without en
and torment ourselves. About your health, abov
everything else, speak frankly to the doctor, in orde
not to be indulged, then let him decide, and liste
to yourself no longer, but obey serenely. It is upo
this which your faithfulness and courage depend:
Without this, you will not have the peace of th
children of God, nor will you deserve to have it.

Endure all the difficulties of your position, whicl
is full of complications and frustration, in the spiri
of penance. These are the penances which God give
you, much more surely than what you would choos
for yourself. There is no place in this world wher
you would not find yourself enjoying some pleasure
Even the most austere solitude would have its diffi
culties. The best state is that one in which the hanc
of God places you. Do not look ahead, and try onl
to accept what comes from moment to moment, ir
the spirit of mortification and of renunciation ol
your own spirit. But this acquiescence should be full
of trust in God, who loves you the more, the less he
spares you. Sleep as much as the doctor considers
necessary for your temperament and your present illness. You should have scruples about your scruples
themselves and not about your sleep. No one, madame, is more sincerely and more respectfully devoted to you than I.

XII

It is a false humility which feels itself unworthy of the kindnesses of God, and dares not await them with confidence. True humility consists in seeing all one's unworthiness, and in living committed to God, having no shadow of a doubt that he can do the greatest things for us. If God, for his works, needed to find foundations already laid in us, we should have reason to believe that our sins had destroyed everything, and that we are unworthy to be chosen by the divine wisdom. But God does not need to find anything in us. He can never find anything in us except what he has put there himself by his grace. One might even say that the nothingness of every creature joined with the sin in an unfaithful soul, is the reason most likely to draw his mercy. It is there that it takes pleasure in flowing in order to manifest itself more vividly. These sinful souls, who have never felt anything in themselves but weakness, can not attribute to themselves any of the gifts of God. It is thus that God chooses the weakest people in the world as St. Paul says, to confound the strongest.

Then have no fear, madame, lest your past infidelities should make you unworthy of God's mercy.

Nothing is so worthy of his mercy as great wretchedness. He came from heaven to earth for sinners, and not for the just. He came to seek for the lost, and all are lost without him. The doctor seeks the sick and not the healthy. O, how God loves those who present themselves bravely before him in their dirtiest and most tattered rags, and who ask him, as their father, for a garment worthy of him! You are waiting for God to show you a gentle and smiling face before you draw close to him, and I, I say that when you open your heart simply to him with entire intimacy, you will not worry any more about the face which he presents to you. If he shows you, as often as he pleases, a severe and exasperated face, let him do so. He never loves so much as when he threatens, for he only threatens to test, to humble, to detach.

Is it the comfort which God gives, or God himself without comfort, which your heart seeks? If it is the comfort, then you do not love God for the love of himself, but for the love of yourself. In that case, you deserve nothing from him. If, on the contrary, you seek God purely, you will find him even more when he tries you than when he comforts you. When he comforts you, you have to be afraid of being more devoted to his consolations than to himself. When he treats you harshly, if you do not cease in the least to remain united to him, it is to him alone that you cling.

Alas, madame, how we deceive ourselves! We become elated by an empty solace, when we are uplifted by a happy experience. We imagine ourselves already carried away to the third heaven, and our feet are not on the ground. But when our faith is dry and bare, then we become discouraged, we think all is lost. In truth, it is then that all is perfected, provided that we do not become discouraged. So let God do his work. It is not for you to regulate the treatment which you should receive. He knows better than you what you need.

You very much deserve a little dryness and testing. Suffer it patiently. God on his side is doing what is right when he rebuffs you. On your side do also what you should, which is to love him without waiting for him to show you any love. Your love will correspond to his. Your confidence will disarm him, and will change all his harshness to endearments. Even though he should not soften at all, you should give yourself up to his just guidance, and adore his purpose to let you die on the cross in abandonment with Jesus his beloved Son. This, madame, is the solid bread of pure faith and generous love, with which you should nourish your soul. I pray God that he will make it strong and active in its trials. Fear nothing. To fear is to lack faith. Await all. All will be given to you. God and his peace will be with you.

Mon. July 24

* This letter, madame, was written two or three days ago. Let me add a word about the news from Ireland. No one shares more than I in your present great anxiety. I pray that God may comfort you, and that he may let you hear better news at the end than at the beginning.

* This postscript refers to the Battle of the Boyne, July 11, 1690. The brother of the Countess served in the army of James II, which was routed.

XIII

Thursday evening (1690)

I know, madame, how deeply you are concerned about affairs in England. Thus I sympathize with the anxiety which you must feel over the reverses of the good cause in Ireland. God knows what he wishes to accomplish, and it is right that we should not know. We must adore his purposes without understanding them. When I heard the bad news, I was afraid that you had some relative in that part of the country, about whom you would be troubled. No sorrow could come to you, madame, without my being deeply affected by it. When you would like me to have the honor of seeing you, simply give me your orders as to the time and place.

XIV

Friday, November 17 (1690)

I am deeply afflicted, madame, by your brothers' misfortunes. But while men abandon them, you must move God to help them by your patience. He is the refuge of the persecuted and the consoler of the afflicted. He has tried you by the things which are happening to your brothers, but he only tries you to detach you, and to make you more worthy of him. *Whoever, he said, loves his father and his mother or his brothers, etc. more than me, is not worthy of me.*

We must sacrifice flesh and blood. You must sacrifice yourself. He is our best friend, and our nearest relation. Alas, madame, what did you expect of men? Didn't you know them? They are weak, inconstant, blind. Some do not desire what they are capable of. Others are not capable of what they desire. The creature is a broken reed. If you wish to lean upon it, the reed bends, can not support you and pierces your hand.

As for your part, this is what I think. God has touched you to the quick in humiliating you. The kind doctor has placed the remedy on the sore and sensitive spot. So much the better. It means that he wishes to heal you. Be still. Adore him who strikes you. Only open your lips to say, *I have well deserved it.*

All talk against the King and Queen would serve but to avenge yourself, without helping you. You would do them harm without doing yourself any good. Thus you can not conscientiously speak, such letting go would be shameful. As for me, I believe that God was caring for you on this occasion. It will turn out for your spiritual advantage. If you lose the fruit of such a cross, you will be doubly unhappy and you will fail God in a very dangerous way. But how much grace comes with this cross, if you carry it bravely! It is by this that you will enter a new way and can hasten toward evangelical perfection. So do not hang back, madame. Bitter as the cup may be, drink it to the dregs, as did Jesus Christ.

I pray him to give you the strength, and not to allow you to give way to the unjust sallies of resentment. Jesus Christ died for those who brought him to death, and he has taught us to love, to bless and to help with our prayers those who curse us and persecute us. Redouble your prayers in this time of trouble and temptation. You will find in the heart of Jesus Christ dying on the cross all that is lacking in your own, in order to love those whom your pride would like to hate and to confound.

XV

Sunday, Nov. 19, (1690)

You can express to your brother, madame, any amount of sadness, pain and even grief over the misfortunes which have come to him. You can add a great eagerness to find harmless ways to help him. You must however avoid showing him resentment against the people who are against him. This would be to embitter his spirit, and to strengthen the passion of hate and vengeance which you should try to soften. Only tell him the exact facts which are necessary for him to understand the continuity of his affairs, and to make decisions in line with his true interest. Do not tell him any circumstances which are only going to poison his heart. You will spare him not only temptations, but much more mental suffering. If you wish to come to-morrow, Monday, to the entresol of madame the Duchess of Beauvilliers, I shall be there at a quarter before eight, after the evening study hour. I should be delighted, madame, to go to pay you my respects at your home, but you would be less free there, and I should be slightly embarrassed to do so.

XVI

Wednesday, April 4, (1691)

I am very sorry, madame, that you are doing so badly, but what consoles me about it, is that you are dissatisfied with yourself. This sincere dissatisfaction is of more value than marvelous behavior, with which one feels well pleased. If you wish me to have the honor of seeing you this evening, I shall be free around six o'clock, and I shall go wherever you tell me to. Although I try to steel you against your sufferings, and even against the discouragement caused by your faults, I am none the less touched by your difficulties.

XVII

Saturday, June 2, (1691)

You would wish me to give up going to you, madame, because of a heavy cold which keeps me in my room. It has not stopped me from projecting a letter which I am sending to you. You will take from it, quite simply please, whatever you think helpful, and you will have no doubt of my good intention. I pray God, not to deliver you from the crosses, if you need them, but to make you carry them with a courage humble and serene. Nature only inspires a courage which is proud, disdainful and irritated by those whom God uses to humiliate us. So be great in God and not in yourself, great by gentleness and patience, small by humility.

XVIII

Versailles, June 17 (1692)

Madame, you always have to endure both other people and yourself. If you only had to endure others, and if you had never experienced in yourself any of the wretchedness which you condemn in the other person, the poor neighbor would seem to you a monster to be exterminated. But God allows you to have much to endure from your haughty, unfair and rebellious temperament, so that you may learn to bear all the provoking qualities in imperfect people. Remember, madame, that self love is insatiable, and always wants to protest. You would have thought yourself too fortunate, a few months ago if anyone had promised you your brother's release, and the joy of seeing him for two days, before he returned to serve his king. All this has come to pass, and, far from thanking God for a so unhoped for grace, you pity yourself for having seen him so little. Take care, that you did not see him too long.

Why are you so exasperated with the King and Queen of England? Perhaps they, for secret reasons, are powerless to do what you wish. Perhaps you are asking for too much. Perhaps they have different ideas from you, because people have prejudiced them. What! Is prejudice in your eyes an unpardonable crime? Is it not a weakness common to man? And where are those who are proof against it, however good their intentions? Have you never been prejudiced about anything? Can you not forgive others for being so? Come back and be human, madame, while waiting for charity to rule your heart. If you can not entirely moderate and restrain yourself, at least humble yourself. Eat your pride without being discouraged. Try to calm yourself in silence before God, as a mother quiets her child sobbing on her knees.

Little by little quiet will return with recollection. If you use the leisure of Dinan to be strict in your reading and prayer, all will go well. Troubles are what you need, and God who loves you, allows for no lack of them. I pray him to add the strength to bear them.

XIX

Versailles, June 23, 1691

I can not be so sympathetic with your grief as I should like to be, madame. I see in it so many signs of mercy and so great a harvest of grace for you, that if nature regrets it, faith ought to rejoice in it. You lose hope, and without hope you find peace by submission and by utter sacrifice. This is precisely as God wishes. He pushes you to this extreme, in order to detach you from all which is not himself. What is there left, but to embrace the cross which he offers you and to allow yourself to be crucified? When he has indeed crucified you he will console you. But he does not act as do creatures who give poisonous consolations in order to feed the venom of self-love. He only consoles after having taken away every resource of a haughty and spoiled nature. The peace which you find in submission, without any outward bettering of your affairs, is a great gift. By it God accustoms you to be disciplined without being broken. Although weak and sensitive nature is depressed, the heart remains supported. It is a peace as pure as it is barren.

The vision of God who is always right toward his creature, and that of your wretchedness, which de-

serves nothing but humiliation and suffering, these
are the bread on which you must feed during this or
deal. You consent to it, but you can not understand
why God strikes the innocent to purify the guilty
Know, madame, that no one is innocent, and no one
can enter into his judgment. How do you know if
the same blow which humiliates you will not also
humiliate your brother under the mighty hand of
God? We must adore his profound decisions with
out understanding them. Perhaps he wishes, by so
many misfortunes, distantly to prepare your brother
to turn firmly towards him. Perhaps one day you
will both rejoice over what now afflicts you. Let God
act, madame. Man can do nothing. When all seems
lost, all is sometimes saved. God is pleased to throw
us and to lift us again from the precipice by his hand
alone. But, whatever he does for your brother, try
yourself to accept the cross and to adore the hand
which brings it to you in order to sanctify you
Happy is he who is ready for everything, who never
says *This is too much*, who counts, not on his self
but on the Almighty, who only wants as much con
solation as God himself wishes to give, and who
nourishes himself by God's pure will!

XX

Versailles, Sept. 9 (1691)

I am mortified, madame, not to have learned until
two hours ago that you have been ill. I was indeed
told that you were in Paris on a regime and taking
certain long treatments, which you had told me that
you wanted to do before the trip to Dinan; but I
had no idea that you were less well than usual, and I
am ashamed to have been so ill informed of matters
in which I take so much interest. I am assured, madame, that we shall have the honor of seeing you at
Fontainebleau, and that in spite of much suffering,
you do not cease to feel that nature is overcoming
the trouble. This is our best hope for you during the
illness, resources for recovery and at the same time,
the fruit of the cross. I pray him who makes you
suffer to give you peace and submission in your misery. How happy we are when we suffer, provided
that we really wish to suffer and to satisfy the justice
of God! What do we not owe to him, and what pain
we should strictly deserve! An eternity of torment
changed into a few rashes! The loss of God, the
rage and despair of demons changed into a tranquil
and short suffering during which we adore with consolation and hope the hand which has struck us in

mercy. Such crosses deserve thanks rather than complaints. These are the graces which a heart must feel, which has been touched by the goodness of God. Had he covered you with leprosy, he still would spare you. The leprosy of pride, of sin and of self-worship, were much more horrible. It is from this that he has cured you.

I can not wait, madame, to ask you at Fontainebleau how you are getting along in the penitence and the retreat in which God has placed you. Those which we choose are nothing. Only God knows how to crucify.

XXI

Versailles, Sept. 17, 1691

I am delighted, madame, to learn that you have regained your health. The feeling with which you tell me so makes it evident that the cross is never without fruit, when it is received in the spirit of sacrifice. I hope, madame, that we shall have the honor of seeing you again at Fontainebleau with a renewal of grace and of detachment from the world. You are right to believe that it is not necessary to wait for freedom and a retreat completely to detach oneself, and to conquer the old man. This free situation is only a beautiful idea. Perhaps we shall never attain it, and we must keep ourselves ready to die in the servitude of our state, if Providence prevents our plan of retreat. You are not your own, and God only asks of you that which depends on yourself. The Israelites in Babylon sighed for Jerusalem, but how many there were of them who never saw Jerusalem again, and who finished their life in Babylon! What an illusion, if they had always waited until the time of their return to their native land to faithfully serve the true God, and to perfect themselves! Perhaps you will do as these Israelites.

What you tell me of Mme. de la Sabliere touches

me and helps me. I have only seen her once, but it made a lasting impression on me. She is indeed right to no longer seek anything from men, having found God, and to give up her best friends. The good friend is within our own heart, the spouse who is jealous and who takes away all the rest. As for death, it only worries carnal and worldly persons. *Perfect love casteth out fear.* It is not by believing ourselves righteous, that we cease to fear. It is simply by loving, and by yielding ourselves to the one we love without a thought of self. That is what makes death sweet and precious. When we are dead to ourselves, the death of the body is only the fulfillment of the work of grace. Since you write to the invalid, madame, won't you be so kind as to tell her how I rejoice according to the faith, in what God has given to her, and how I hope that all her troubles will be blessings?

XXII

Thurs. Sept. 20 (1691)

If you would like to, madame, come soon, at about seven o'clock to the Duchess of Chevreuse's. I trust that she will receive us hospitably, although I have not yet set foot within her door. You see by that, madame, that I am no less rude to her than to you. I am no longer even that to you, it seems to me. Your troubles have taken away my unsociable humor.

XXIII

Versailles, Nov. 15, (1691)

It is a long time, madame, since I paid my respects to you, but I have constantly asked news of you of all who could tell me any, and have talked of your affliction with those who care. God has given you a hard cross in the illness which you suffer. It is stubborn. It is painful. Besides the pains of the illness, you have those of the remedies. But the pain is not what hurts you the most. You are brave and firm enough with yourself to suffer patiently. But God has taken you by another more sensitive place, which is your weakness. He attacks your delicacy and your daintiness. You who have a so exquisite and so supercilious taste, you are reduced to being disgusted with yourself and to fearing that you are disgusting to others. It is God who does this, and all that he does is good, and all that he does is in mercy. He has to crush out our self-love and our pride. Let us adore his hand, humble ourselves. I pray him, madame, to give you, both for body and spirit, all that his goodness is bound to bestow upon you.

XXIV

Friday, Nov. 30, 1691

I understand, madame, that the eloquence of the Count of Gramont has done more than you had dared hope for, for your brother's liberty. Allow me to express my joy over this in this note, while waiting until in some entresol, or near the little white marble fire-place, I can tell you how deeply I share in this happy outcome.

XXV

I shall have difficulty, madame, in remembering the things which I said to you last Sunday. All that I have kept in my mind, it seems to me, is that I told you two things, first, that we ought to sacrifice ourselves in the state in which Providence has placed us, without making plans or patterns of virtue for the future; and second, that we ought to have a very great faithfulness to God in the smallest things.

Most people pass the better part of their life in knowing and regretting their manner of living, in proposing to change it, in making rules for free time which they hope to have and which often is not given to them, and thus in losing in resolutions the time which they ought to be using to perform good deeds, and to work profitably towards their salvation.

We must, madame, regard such notions as a very dangerous temptation. Our salvation is the task of every day and every moment of our life. There is no better time to work for it than that which God gives us now, in his mercy, because we have today, and perhaps we shall have no tomorrow. Salvation does not come by wishing for it, but by working for it with all the best in us. The uncertainty in which we live ought to make us realize that our will should be centered on this one concern, and that every other occupation is unworthy of us, since it does not lead us to God, who should be the end of all our actions, and who is the God of our salvation, which is the name that David often gives him in the Psalms.

Why, madame, do we make plans for perfection? It is because we believe them necessary to save us. Why then do we put off carrying out these plans, since it is as necessary that we work for our salvation today as ten years from now, at the court as well as in a more retired life? We must always be on the safe side in this matter of our salvation, in which we lose all or gain all. The state of life to which God has called us is sure for us, when we fulfill all our duties therein. If God had foreseen that at the courts of princes we could not win salvation, he would have commanded us never to stay there. Far from having given us such a command, it is he who makes kings and who rules their courts, and who permits that birth or the duties which we have there, give us entry to them. Yet he wishes us to be saved there, and that we should there find the road which leads to heaven, which consists in devotion to the truth, to that truth, I say, which Jesus Christ has told us would deliver us, that is to say, would keep us from all of the dangers to which we are exposed in this world.

The more of these you meet, madame, in the state in which you are, the more also you should watch yourself, lest you yield to them. To watch oneself, is to be attentive to God. It is to have him always present. It is to withdraw into oneself. It is not to be weakened or distracted willingly among his creatures. It is to love as much as one can, the retreat, the holy books and prayer. It is to expand, as the Prophet said, one's heart in the presence of God. It is to find him in one's self. It is to seek him by the fervor of one's desires. It is to love him more than all things, and to avoid all that we know is displeasing to him. This virtue, madame, is the virtue of every state. It is a wonderful relief at court, and I know nothing which can help us more not to love the world, in the midst of the world, than the use which we know how to make of this virtue. Then make yourself familiar with it, madame, and try never to forget that you are with God, and that God is in you, so that you keep yourself always faithful in his service.

Accustom yourself often to adore his holy will by a humble submission of your own to his commandments and his providence. Pray that he may sustain you, lest you should fall. Beg him to accomplish his

work in you, and, having given you the desire to save
yourself in the state in which you are, beg him that
you may indeed save yourself in the state in which
he has placed you. He does not ask great things of
you for your success. *The kingdom of God is within
you.* This is what Jesus Christ tells us in his Gospel.
We meet with it there when we wish to. Let us do
that which we know he does ask of us; but when we
do know his will, let us not spare ourselves at all, and
let us be very faithful to him. This fidelity ought not
only to compel us to do great things for his service,
and for our salvation, but all those things which
come up casually, as part of our position. If we only
saved ourselves by great actions, there would be few
people who could hope to be saved. Salvation is re-
lated to the will of God which we should fulfill. The
smallest things become great when God asks them of
us. They are only small in themselves. They are always great when they are done for God, when they
lead us to God, and when they serve us as a means to
possess him forever.

Remember, madame, that he has said to us in the
Gospel that he who would be unfaithful in little
things would also be so in great ones; and that he
who would be faithful in the least things would be
also in the most important. It seems to me that a
soul which desires to be sincerely devoted to God

never questions whether a matter is small or great It is enough for it to know that the one for love of whom it is acting is infinitely great, and that he de serves to have every creature solely occupied in giving him the glory which is his due, and which is only given by fulfilling his will.

For yourself, madame, I think that you ought to accept your troubles as your principal penitence The importunities of the world should detach you from yourself. Bear in peace this constant burden and you will not cease to advance in the narrow way It is narrow because of the pain which wrings the heart, but it is large because of the stretch which God gives to the heart from within. We suffer, we are surrounded by adversity, we are deprived of ever spiritual consolations; but we are free, because we want everything which we have, and we should no want to be released from it. We endure our own weakness, and we prefer it to the most pleasant cir cumstances, because it is God's choice. The grea point is to suffer without being discouraged.

XXVI

The Advent season should inspire us, madame, with a great desire to give ourselves to God, and to prepare our hearts to receive the fullness of his grace, and to make us ready to be born again with Jesus Christ, or, to put it better, to profit by the fruits of his birth by the union which we should have with him, and which only the love of God can form in us.

We should believe that each one of us is told separately, that which St. John said long ago to the Jews, to stir them to repentance. *Prepare ye the way of the Lord. Make his paths straight.* So will he find our hearts ready to receive him and to distribute his blessings.

This preparation of the heart consists in an ardent desire to possess him. This is why holy church makes us remember during this season the holy patriarchs who sighed for the coming of the Messiah, who, for that reason, is called in the Holy Scriptures the *Desired,* or the *Desire of all peoples.* We stir these desires in ourselves in prayer, when we open our hearts in the presence of God, and when we beg him to come to take possession of us. Jesus Christ himself has taught us this manner of prayer, when he commanded us to ask of his Father that his Kingdom come, meaning that he reign tranquilly within us, and that we be bound by love to his laws and to his Gospel. We can not form these desires within us better anywhere than in solitude. Therefore, madame, I do advise you to withdraw yourself as often and for as long as you can, to draw upon yourself the graces of God, resting assured that, as God long ago made John the Baptist hear his voice in the desert, and as it was in such places far away from the crowds of the world, that he gave people the knowledge of the Messiah, he will also enlighten you and fill you with the grace of his spirit, when, in retreat, you try to concentrate on him, and pray him to let you share in his merit.

I think then, madame, that it is right for you to spend much time in prayer, and that you take for the subject of your devotions the third chapter of St. Matthew, part of the first chapter of St. Mark, the third of St. Luke, and the first of St. John. You will find there the subjects of the exhortations of St. John the Baptist to the people, which contain what we ought to do to prepare ourselves to profit by the coming of Jesus Christ into the world and into our hearts.

We can reduce everything which he has said to the following things.

1. Penitence, which should make us withdraw

from the world, weep that we could have been so attached to it, and embrace the teachings of the Gospel in order to walk in the narrow way.

2. Profound humility, feeling ourselves unworthy to appear before Jesus Christ, still more so to unite ourselves with him and to receive him in our hearts.

3. A great courage and an unbreakable firmness for the good, never being discouraged by seeing the difficulties involved, and resisting vigorously the currents of the world.

XXVII

I assure you, madame, that the letter which you have done me the honor of writing me has given me real joy. I learn by it that you are better, that you are to return here at the beginning of the year, and what is still better, that you have tried to make good use of your crosses. That which strikes at your supersensitiveness and your scornful fastidiousness goes right to the mark. God knows well how to choose what we need, and all the blows which he gives us are in mercy. Your illness is of more good to you than all the natural talents which have attached you to the world. You are very fortunate to be making this penance. It should teach you to despise nothing, to be horrified by nothing, not to prefer yourself to anyone, to bear the wretchedness of others. The leprosy of pride, of self-love, and of all the other passions of the mind, if we were not blind, would appear to us much more horrible and more contagious than the most loathsome diseases, which only disfigure the flesh. I am waiting, madame, with a sincere impatience for your return. To no one will it mean more, nor has any one more respect for you.

XXVIII

Friday, March 21, (1692)

It is not I, madame, who am hard to see. It is you.
Remember this, and stop scolding against the people
who consider me a relic. I should not dare to go to
seek you with the Count of Gramont and all those
other people who give you such good company.

To speak very seriously, I am sorry for your difficulties. You must have some free hours or you can not
recollect yourself. Try to save them, and consider
that these little scraps of your days are the best of all.
Above all, madame, save your morning, and defend
it as one defends a besieged place. Make vigorous
sorties against those who bother you. Clean out the
trench, and then shut yourself up again in your
dungeon. Until after dinner is too long, not to have
a breathing space.

Recollection is the one remedy for your pride, for
the bitterness of your scornful criticism, for the
sallies of your imagination, for your impatience with
those who serve you, for your love of pleasure, and
for all your other faults. The remedy is excellent,
but it needs to be frequently renewed. You are a
good watch but one whose coil is short and which
has to be rewound often. Take up again the read-

ings which have touched you. They will touch you again, and you will get more out of them than the first time. Bear with yourself without flattering yourself or becoming discouraged. This happy medium is rarely found. We promise ourselves great things of ourselves and of our good intentions, or else we despair of all. Hope for nothing from yourself. Look for everything to God. Despair of our own weakness, which is incorrigible, and unlimited confidence in the power of God, are the true foundations of every spiritual edifice. When you will not have much time to yourself, do not miss making use of the least moments which do remain yours. It does not take much time to love God, to renew yourself in his presence, to lift your heart to him, or to adore him from the depths of your heart, to offer to him what you are doing and what you are suffering. This is the true Kingdom of God within us, which nothing can trouble.

XXIX

I can not, madame, learn of the continued illness of the Count of Gramont, without letting you know how I share in your anxiety. It comes at a time when you would seem to have more need of comfort than of suffering and trials, but God alone knows what you need, and we can only let him act at the expense of nature. I hope then, madame, that he will double your patience and courage so that you can help the invalid, and satisfy his every need. Those of the body are not the greatest, and I pray God to give you words strong enough to place the truths of salvation in his heart. No one will ever be, madame, more sincerely nor more respectfully devoted to you than I.

XXX

Tuesday, Nov. 4, 1692

You should have no doubt, madame, of what is your consolation in your troubles. It is God who wants to make them serve to detach you from yourself and from the comforts of life. Recollection and fervor would be less apt to reduce your superciliousness, and to crucify your too delicate sensibilities. By your own choice turn always to reading, to prayer, to solitude and to silence. Hold firm. Cut yourself short, especially in the evening, in order to have a more free morning, but when Providence draws you into inevitable complications, do not be upset. You will find God wherever he has led you, in the utmost confusion, as in the most tranquil prayer. You will find there nourishment within, and mortification of yourself. When the ladies of whom you speak are here, I shall be delighted to have them give me the honor of seeing you. Meanwhile I pray God with all my heart, that he may be your light in your present situation. Truly, madame, I think of you often, and of the grace which you need, even when you perhaps think that I do not give you a thought. Nothing could surpass my devotion to you.

XXXI

Versailles, Wed. Nov. 12, 1692

I am delighted, madame, at the good news which you graciously give me of the Count of Gramont. I hope for him more than ever, a long and happy life, since he thinks seriously of making good use of it. If I felt that I could see him without inconveniencing him, I should try to free myself one of these days in the interlude between our morning and evening studies, in order to congratulate him on his good intentions. But I should not want to go to urge him to hasten in the steps of others, nor to seem to preach. Besides, I do not even know if my health will allow it, because it has been bad enough for the past fort-night. So, please have the kindness, madame, to find out quietly how the Count feels, without involving me. He has all the best help which you could hope for him. If I made this trip, it would not be for his need, but to show you my zeal, and simply to have the honor of seeing you both together. Write me frankly what you think about this.

As for you, madame, you have only to bear your cross patiently. The troublesome things which you think come between God and yourself, will be but the means of uniting you to him, if you suffer them humbly. The things which overwhelm us, and which confound our pride, yet do us more good than the things which draw us apart and inspire us. You need more than others to be overcome, like St. Paul at the gates of Damascus, and to find yourself at the end of your own resources. The deeper the wound, the greater and more painful must be the incision. All that you are suffering is the operation of the hand of God, who wishes to cure you of a disease which you were not feeling, and which is a thousand times greater than those of which nature complains. Pride is more repulsive than your abscesses, and you have no horror of it. Do not lose courage, madame. Yield yourself to the hand of God, who strikes you in mercy, without by your troubles, and within by the illness. He loves you, and wishes you to love him with Jesus Christ on the cross. Turn to him for everything, and you will receive according to the measure of your faith.

XXXII

I was very sorry, madame, not to have the honor of seeing you, when you came here the last time. I hope that the good health of the Count of Gramont will allow you to return soon, and to stay longer. This good health is, they say, excellent. It is the gift of God, and it would not be right to use it against him. The Count will have to have a clear and honorable behavior toward God, as he always has had toward the world. True noblesse demands loyalty, firmness and constancy. A man so grateful to the King, who only gives perishable benefits, would he wish to be ungrateful and unfaithful to God, who gives all? I could not believe it, and I do not wish even to think of it. I believe that I have seen his good heart, and I hope for him courage to despise malicious reproaches and cold ridicule. You know better than anyone, madame, how to warn him against the ways and unconscious involvements of society. He should consider seriously that his recovery, which delays his death, only delays it for a little while, and that the longest life will always be short. For myself, as I do not want at all to preach, I limit myself to rejoicing with you, madame, in this happy recovery. I can't wait to have the honor of seeing you both here in complete health, and with the same attitudes.

XXXIII

I thank you very humbly, madame, for sharing this letter with me. It is good and touching. I like his humility and his lack of confidence in himself, even better than his fervency. So long as he takes no steps, even for good, except by advice of a holy and experienced person, all will go marvelously, but a good deed is no longer a good deed when a person performs it in his own fashion. The first and the only solid good is utter renunciation of one's own will and one's own judgment. I am sorry for you in this difficult situation but if you remain faithful to all that you can, God himself will supply what you can not perform, by the continual constraint in which his providence is placing you. What I hope most for you, is humility and simplicity of spirit. I fear for you a glowing, lofty devotion, which seeming to go deeply into reading and practice, nourishes in secret a suspicion of grandeur, quite contrary to Jesus Christ the little child, simple and scorned by the wise of his century. You must be a child with him. I pray him with all my heart, madame, to take away from you not only your faults, but also the taste for greatness in virtue, and to make you small by his grace.

XXXIV

The crosses which we fashion for ourselves, by an uneasy anticipation of the future, these are not the crosses which come from God. We tempt him by our false wisdom, by wishing to foresee his plan, and by forcing ourselves to supplement his providence with our own providence. The fruit of our wisdom is always bitter, and God allows it to confound us, when we leave his fatherly guidance. The future is not yet for us. Perhaps it never will be. If it comes, perhaps it will come quite differently than we had expected. Then let us close our eyes on that which God hides from us, and on that which he holds in reserve in the treasury of his deep wisdom. Let us worship without seeing. Let us be still. Let us remain in peace.

The crosses of the present moment always bring with them their grace, and consequently their amelioration. We see in them the hand of God which is making itself felt. But the crosses of uneasy anticipation are seen outside of God's plan. We see them without the grace to endure them. We see them even with an unfaithfulness which alienates grace. Thus everything about them is bitter and unbearable. Everything is black. Everything is without help. And the soul which has wanted for curiosity's sake to taste the forbidden fruit, finds only death and rebellion within herself and no comfort.

You see what it means, not to trust God, and to dare to violate his secret, of which he is jealous. *Sufficient unto each day*, says Jesus Christ, *is the evil thereof*. The evil of each day becomes a good when we let God act. Who are we to say to him, *Why do you do that?* He is the Lord and that is enough. He is the Lord. May he do all that is good in his eyes. Though he elevate or though he abase, though he strike or though he console, though he crush or though he heal every wound, though he give death or life, he is always the Lord. We are only the work and consequently the plaything of his hands. What does it matter, so long as he is glorified and that his will is accomplished in us? Let us get outside of ourselves. No more self-interest, and the will of God, which is being evolved every moment in all things, will comfort us also every moment in all that God will bring to pass around us, or within us at the expense of ourselves. The contradictions of men, their inconstancy, even their injustices, will show themselves to be the effects of the wisdom, justice and invariable goodness of God. We shall see only God, infinitely good, who conceals himself in the weaknesses of blind and corrupt men.

Thus this deceiving face of the world, which passes like a shifting scene, will become a very real thing to us and worthy of eternal praise to God. Men, great as they may seem, are nothing in themselves. But how great is God in them! It is he who makes use of the strange whim, the bitter pride, the dissimulation, the vanity, and all the mad passions, in the eternal plan which he has for his elect. He uses the within and the without, the corruption of other men, our own imperfections, and our own sensitiveness, in a word, he uses everything for our own sanctification. He moves heaven and earth. Nothing is done except to purify us and to make us worthy of him. Let us rejoice then, when our heavenly Father tests us here below with various temptations, interior and exterior, when he makes everything go wrong without, and makes all painful within. Let us rejoice, because it is by such pains that our faith, more precious than gold, is purified. Let us rejoice to experience thus the nothingness and the lie of all that is not God; because it is by this crucifying experience that we are torn away from ourselves and from the desires of our time. Let us rejoice, because it is by such birth pains that the new man is born in us.

What! We become discouraged, and it is the hand of God who hastens to accomplish his work!

That is what we have always been hoping that he
would do, and as soon as he begins to do it, we worry.
Our cowardice and our impatience halt the hand of
God. I say that we experience in the troubles of life,
the emptiness and the deceit of all that is not God.
The emptiness because there is an infinite void in
all which is not the infinite good and the only good.
Furthermore, we find there deceit. The creature
promises much and he lies. The nothing appears to
be something, but it is only an empty bluff. What
does it not make us hope! But, in the end, what
does it give? Vanity and mental affliction every-
where under the sun, but above all, in the highest
places.

Emptiness is no less emptiness there, because it
is equally nothing anywhere. But it is more of a
liar there. It is a decoration which is no less hollow,
but which is more trimmed up. It lights our hopes.
It stirs our desires. But it never fills our heart. That
which is emptiness itself can not fill anything. Those
weak and unhappy creatures who are the divinities
of the earth, can not give the strength and the hap-
piness which they do not have. Is a person going to
draw water from a dry fountain? No, of course not!
Why then wish to go to draw peace and joy at the
houses of those great ones, whom we see sigh, and
who themselves beg for amusement, and whom bore-

dom comes to consume in the midst of all the ap-
pearance of pleasure? May they become like those
who put their trust in them, as the Prophet said of
those who worshipped idols. Let us place our hopes
higher, and in a place more inaccessible to the acci-
dents of this life.

In short, I have said that vanity and falsehood are
found in all which is not God, thus they are also
found in ourselves. Nothingness! Alas, what is so
empty and such a vacuum as our heart? Falsehood!
What do we not promise ourselves? But our promises are full of falsehood. Happy he who is ever un-
deceived by them. Our heart is as vain and as false
as all that is most corrupt outside of it. Let us by no
means distrust the world without distrusting ourselves. We are more untrustworthy than it, since,
having received more from God, we are more ungrateful and more unfaithful. Let us agree that the
world by a secret justice, deceives us, fails us and
treats us badly, as we have wanted to deceive God, as
we have failed him, as we have so many times done
harm to the spirit of grace. The more the world
disgusts us, the more it will advance the work of
God, and it will do us as much good, in wanting to
do us harm, as it would have done us harm if we
had received all the false blessings which it seemed
about to give us.

I pray God, madame, that your faith be fed every day on these truths, that they germinate in your heart, that they put forth deep roots there, and above all that they help you to renew yourself in the mind of Jesus Christ during your retreat. *May the peace of God, said St. Paul, which passeth all understanding, keep your hearts and thoughts in Jesus Christ.* Let us cut off every root of bitterness, and let us throw away all sadness which disturbs the peace and the simple trust of the children of God. Let us turn towards our Father in all our troubles. Let us bury ourselves in his so tender breast, where we can lack nothing. Let us rejoice in hope, and taste, far from the world and the flesh, the pure joy of the Holy Spirit. May our faith be immovable in the midst of storms. Let us hold fast to the great word of the Apostle, *Everything turns to good for those who love God, and for those whom he has chosen according to his good pleasure.*

XXXV

Wed. Nov. 17 (1694)

I think, madame, that you should try, without any great effort, to center your thoughts on God every time that the desire for recollection, and the regret not to be able to practice it touches your heart. It is not necessary to wait for free hours, when we can close the door and not see anyone. The moment which makes us regret recollection can make us practice it. Then and there turn your heart toward God in a simple, familiar and trustful way. All of the most broken moments are good, not only in couch or chair, but even while dressing, doing your hair, even eating, and while listening to others talk. Pointless and boring stories, instead of wearying you, will sustain you, by giving you intervals. Instead of exciting your mockery, they will give you the freedom to recollect yourself. Thus all turns to profit for those who seek God.

Another important rule is to abstain from a fault, every time that you see it before committing it, and to bear the shame of it bravely, if you do not see it until after it has been committed. If you see it before doing it, be sure to keep from resisting the spirit of God, which is warning you within, and which you hear. It is delicate. It is jealous. It wants to be heard and followed. If you grieve it, it retires. The slightest resistance injures it. May everything in you yield to it, as soon as it makes itself felt. The faults of haste or of frailty are nothing in comparison to those which make a person deaf to the secret voice of the Holy Spirit, which is beginning to speak in the depths of the soul.

As for the faults which are not noticed until after they have been committed, the fretting and vexation of self-love never mends them. On the contrary, this vexation is only an impatience of pride at the sight of what mortifies it. The only thing to do with our faults then, is to humiliate ourselves on their account in peace. I say in peace, because it is not being humiliated, if we take our humiliation with chagrin and reluctance. We must condemn our fault, without seeking its softening by any excuse, and see ourselves before God without confusion, without being bitter against ourselves and without being discouraged, but profiting quietly by the humiliation of our fault. Thus one draws from the snake itself the antidote to cure the poison of his bite. The confusion of sin, when it is received in a soul which does not bear it impatiently, is the remedy for sin itself. But it is not being humble, to resist humiliation.

A little of the presence of God during a meal, especially when they are long, and often leisurely, will help much to keep you within the limits of moderation, and to fortify you against your excessive sensitiveness. There are also certain moments at the table, when the first hunger makes people talk little. Then one can, while eating, think a little of God. But all this should only be done as occasion offers and as good taste allows without straining.

There is another thing which I admit troubles me, and which we did not mention today, but we must take it up the next time that I have the honor of seeing you. You will easily understand it. I am very convinced that you ought to exercise extreme firmness against yourself, and to distrust your best intentions. Perhaps you will stop all the blessings which God is preparing for you. Often all that we offer to God is not at all what he wants. What he wants the most from us, is that which we want less to give him, and which we fear he may ask of us. It is Isaac, the only son, the well beloved son, that he wishes to have sacrificed without mercy. All the rest is nothing in his eyes, and he allows all the rest to work out in a painful and fruitless way, because his benediction is not upon the work of a divided soul. He wants all and to the point of peace. *Who is it,* says Scripture, *who has resisted God and has been able to be in peace?* If you wish to be, and if you wish to obtain

God's blessing on your labors, hold nothing back. Cut to the quick, burn, spare nothing, and the God of peace will be with you. What consolation, what liberty, what force, what enlargement of the heart, what increase of grace, when we leave nothing more between God and self, and when we have made unhesitatingly the last sacrifices! I pray our Lord, and I shall pray every day, madame, to give you the courage to do this.

XXXVI

I do not remember very well, madame, what I was talking about, and what you have told me to write, but it seems to me that it was a question of the too great sensitiveness which we feel within ourselves, and which we can not overcome. Plenty of people are tormented and chagrined on this account.

This sensitiveness does not depend on us. God has given it to us with our temperament to train us. He does not want to free us from it, but to use it, on the contrary to overwhelm us. So let us enter into his plans. We need temptations. It is only a question of not yielding to them. Those from within are like those from without. They all tend to lead us to victory through struggle. The temptations from within are still more useful in that they serve more directly to humiliate us by the experience of our inner corruption. Those without only go to show the wickedness of the world which surrounds us. Those within make us feel that we are as depraved in our inclinations as even the world. Then let us bear our inward insurrections with a humble confidence and an unruffled peace, and all the temptations of our own depths, as well as the storms which come from other creatures. All comes equally from the hand of

God, who knows how to use us as well as others, to make us die to ourselves.

It is often pride which disturbs us, and which makes us discouraged to see so many stubborn revolts within, while it would like to see all passions overcome, in order to feed itself on the glory of it and to delight in our own perfection. Let us try to be faithful from the depths of our wills, despite the repugnances and disturbances of our natures, and let us allow God to act, when he wishes to show us by these tempests to what shipwrecks we should be exposed, if his powerful hand did not preserve us. Even if we happen to fall voluntarily from frailty, then let us humble ourselves, let us annihilate ourselves, let us correct ourselves without pity for ourselves. Let us not lose a moment in turning again towards God, but let us do so simply and easily. Let us raise ourselves and take the right course again bravely, without being grieved or discouraged by our fall.

XXXVII

As long as we stay wrapped up in ourselves, we are exposed to the contrariness of men, to their wickedness and to their injustice. Our humor exposes us to that of others. Our passions clash with those of our neighbors. Our desires as well are spots where we lay ourselves open to all the shots of the rest of mankind. Our pride, which is incompatible with the pride of our neighbor, rises like the waves of a troubled sea. Everyone opposes us, every one repels us, every one attacks us. We are open on every side by the sensitiveness of our passions and by the jealousy of our pride. There is no peace to be hoped for in ourselves, when we live at the mercy of a host of avid and insatiable desires, when we could never satisfy this me, so hard to please and so easily offended by everything which affects us.

Thus it is that in our personal relations we are like sick people who have languished a long time in one bed. There is no part of the body which can be touched without wounding them. The person ill of self-centeredness, and pitying himself, can not be touched without uttering loud cries. Touch him with a finger tip, he thinks himself skinned. Join to this hyper-sensitiveness the tactlessness of a neighbor, full of imperfections which he does not know himself, join to it the reaction of the neighbor to our own faults, which are no less great because they are our reaction to his, and you have all the children of Adam becoming each other's torment. You have one half of mankind made miserable by the other half, and making it miserable in its turn. In every nation, in every city, in every community, in every family, and between two friends, you have the martyrdom of self-centeredness.

The one remedy then is to go out of one's self to find peace. We must renounce self and lose all self interest in order to have nothing to lose, nor to fear, nor to be concerned about. Then does one enjoy the true peace reserved for men of good will, that is to say for those who have no other will than that of God, which becomes theirs. Then can men have no more power over us, because they can neither take us by our desires nor by our fears. Then we wish all things and we do not wish anything. This is to be inaccessible to the enemy. This is to be invulnerable. Man can only do what God gives him to do, and everything which God gives him to do against us being the will of God, is also our own will.

In this state, one has set his treasure so high, that no hand can reach it to take it away from us. Someone will take away our reputation, but we consent to it, because we know how good it is to be humiliated when God humiliates us. We meet with disappointment in friendship. So much the better. It is the one true friend who is jealous of all the others, and who detaches us from them to purify our attachments. We are pestered, tied down, frustrated, but God is doing it and that is enough. We love the hand which crushes us. Peace is found in all these troubles, the joyful peace which follows us all the way to the cross! We want what we have. We want nothing which we have not. The more perfect this abandon, the more profound the peace. If some attachment and some desire remains, the peace is only a half peace. If every tie were broken, freedom would be boundless. What if disgrace, suffering, death come to burst upon me, I hear Jesus Christ who says to me, *Fear not those who kill the body, and who then can do nothing more.* O, how weak they are, even when they take away life! How short their power is! They can only break an earthen pot, only kill what is dying by itself every day, only advance a little that death which is a deliverance, after which we escape from their hands into the bosom of God, where all is serene and changeless.

XXXVIII

I have wanted for a long time, madame, to stir your memory, and to have the honor of writing to you, but you know that life passes in good desires without effect, in matters even more important than social duties. So my good purpose has been, madame, to ask you how things are, and many horrid little hindrances have always taken my freedom to do so. However, I have not been ignorant of your whereabouts, because the Count of Gramont has told me. If Bourbon is as good for you as it is for him, I shall not be surprised if it makes you forget the court. Bourbon is for him the true fountain of youth, into which I believe he plunges night and morning. Versailles does not rejuvenate in this way. Here one must have a smiling face, but the heart smiles but little.

However little remains of personal desires and sensibilities, there is always something to watch out for here. No one has what he wants. He has what he would rather not have. He is grieved over his bad luck, and sometimes over the good luck of others. He despises the people with whom he spends his time, and he curries their favor. He is pestered, and he would be very upset not to be and to live in solitude. There are a swarm of little hovering cares, which come every morning as you wake, and which do not leave you again until evening. They come in relays to annoy you. The more a person is in favor, the more he is at the mercy of these imps. This is what is called life in the world, and the object of envy of fools. However these fools are the whole blind human race. Every man who does not know God who is all, and the nothingness of all the rest, is one of those fools who admire and envy a very unhappy state. The sage also has said that, *the number of fools is infinite.* I hope with all my heart, madame, that you have the good spirit which God gives, as it is written in the gospels, to all those who ask it of him. This remedy, which heals the heart, is preferable to the waters which only heal the body. We must think of rejuvenating ourselves in Jesus Christ for the life eternal, and allow this outer man to grow old, who is, according to St. Paul, the body of sin. This is too long a sermon. Forgive it, please, madame, to a man who has long kept silence.

Fr. de Fénelon, n. Arch. de Cambrai

XXXIX

I can not have the honor of going to you, madame, because the young princes' studies are about to begin. I wish you a happy journey, perfect health, complete forgetting of all the troubles which you are leaving, and as many consolations as I have crosses! I pray that God may sanctify you, and that he may overwhelm you with his blessings. Be sure, madame, that all my life long, I shall keep a respectful devotion to you.

XL

Cambrai, Sept. 12, 1697

I have always been deeply conscious, madame, of the evidences of your goodness. You may judge whether my appreciation lessens, when you redouble your attentions so kindly in circumstances in which the rest of the world forgets. It is pure love to love people who are no longer in favor. Interested love is the kind at court. It is in the world that one hears more evil, and where one should better understand this distinction. I am delighted, madame, that you are pleased with the Duchess of Beauvilliers. She is truly good, and wishes in good faith to overcome in herself everything which is less Christ-like. She warmly returns your feelings toward her.

I am here in the hope and the submission of a child of the church, who ought to be more submissive to it than anyone else, because he owes more to the church because of his position, and because he is not worthy to be a shepherd unless he is himself a docile lamb. If I am mistaken, I shall be the one who will gain the most from this affair because I shall be set right. The truth is far more important than a triumph.

I can not end, madame, without begging you to

tell the Count of Gramont that I shall never in my life forget that he did not blush for me, and that he acknowledged me without embarrassment before the courtiers at Marly. He will not understand these words unknown at court, but you will be good enough to explain them to him. Allow me to speak also, madame, of the good company which I left in your apartment the last time. They are people whom I like and honor. It is only you, madame, who will not receive any compliment from me. I content myself with wishing you a heart humbled under the hand of God and softened towards your neighbor, a mind simple as a dove and wise as a serpent, to avoid everything which can corrupt you, finally a true detachment from the world and from yourself, the practice of which may be real and constant. All goes well with us, when we go forward in this way, because it is the one and only way for us. Success, reputation, favor, talent, comforts, are only delusions.

Letters to a Soldier

The soldier to whom these letters are addressed is thought to be Jules-Armand Colbert, the Marquis of Blainville, son of Leon Baptiste Colbert the brilliant and ruthless adviser of Louis XIV, and brother of the Duchess of Beauvilliers. He was made a Colonel in 1684 when he was twenty. His father had a breviary printed for the use of his household. The habit of reciting the divine office was fairly common at that time even among the ladies and gentlemen of the court.

I

You have forgotten me, monsieur, but it is not in my power to do the same to you. I carry something in the depths of my heart which always speaks of you to me, and which makes me always eager to ask for news of you. I felt this particularly during the perils of your campaign. Your forgetfulness, far from rebuffing me, touches me still more. You showed me formerly a sort of friendship which leaves a lasting impression, and which softens me nearly to tears, when I recall our conversations. I hope that you remember how sympathetic and heart-felt they were.

Have you found since then anything dearer than God, when one is worthy of feeling his presence? Do the truths which enraptured you, do so no more? Has the pure light of the kingdom of God been extinguished? Can the emptiness of the world have received a new value? Is what used to be only a bad dream, one no longer?

This God to whose breast you were turning your heart, and who was making you taste a peace above all human feeling, is he no longer kind? The eternal beauty, always new for pure eyes, has it no charm for you? The source of the heavenly joys, of the pleasures without remorse, which are in the Father of mercies and the God of all comfort, has this source dried up? No, because he is putting in my heart a too pressing desire to recall you to him. I can not resist it. I have hesitated a long time, and have said to myself, *I will only irritate him.* In beginning this letter, even, I made myself rules of discretion, but at the fourth line my heart escaped me. Should you not answer me at all, should you find me absurd, I shall not cease to speak of you to God with grief, being no longer able to speak to you yourself. Once more, monsieur, forgive me, if I go beyond every rule. I see it as well as you, but I feel myself pushed and led. God has not forgotten you by any means, because he is acting in me so poignantly for your safety.

Why does he ask for you, except that you wanted to be happy? Have you not felt that a person is so, when he is loving him? Have you not realized that without him one can not truly be so, whatever release he goes seeking in the pleasures of the senses? Then since you do know where the fountain of life is, and since you in other days have plunged your heart in it to quench its thirst, why do you still look for uncovered and contaminated wells? O, beautiful days, O, happy days, which were only lighted by the gentle rays of a loving compassion! When will you return? When will it be given me to see again this dear child of God recalled under his powerful hand, overwhelmed with his favors and with the delights of his sacred feast, giving joy to all heaven, treading the earth beneath his feet, and drawing from the realization of human frailty an inexhaustible source of humility and of ardor?

I am not going to tell you, monsieur, what you have to do. God himself will tell you according to your needs, if you listen to him within, and if you bravely avoid worthless people. But finally, he wants you. Follow him. What can we refuse to him who wishes to give us all things, in giving us himself? So, monsieur, do everything which you would like to do, but love God, and may his love revived in you be your only guide. I have often thanked him for having protected you from the perils of the campaign, where your soul was even more exposed than your body. Often I have trembled for you. End my fears. Give me again the joy of my heart. I can never feel a greater one than to be again with you, making only one heart and one soul in the house of God, while looking forward to our joyous hope, and the glorious coming of the great God, who will intoxicate us with the flood of his pure delights. Your ears are not yet unaccustomed to the sublime language of truth. Your heart is made to feel its charms. This is the delicious bread which we eat every day at our Father's table. Why have you left it?

With such sustenance you should not fear the need of any other things, but there is one last appeal which I want to make to you. Even though you should not feel the strength to return to the happy state in which you used to be, at least answer me, at least do not run away from me. I know what it is to be weak. I am a thousand times more so than you. It is very useful to have realized that we are. But do not add to the weakness inseparable from humanity, estrangement from that which can diminish it. You shall be in charge of our correspondence. I shall never speak to you except of what you would surely like to hear. I shall keep the secret of God in my heart, and I shall always be, monsieur, with affection and complete respect, etc.

II

I was deeply sorry, monsieur, to find you gone when I returned from my little trip. But those who know that God does all, believe that he does all for the best. I pray him with all my heart to give you as much courage to withstand the judgments of the world, as he has given you to withstand the perils of war. Is it not a strange folly in men, not to fear the blows which can kill them at any moment, and perhaps damn them, while they are so timid and so weak to withstand a cold mockery, or the criticism of even those people whom they scorn the most?

Thus ambition, that is to say love empassioned by a phantom, makes men fearless in the midst of the greatest dangers, while the hope in Almighty God, and the expectation of his eternal Kingdom, can not reassure them against the idle talk of a shocking ungodliness. O, how weak and cowardly they are, those men who pride themselves on having such strong hearts and on being so brave! It is only by the intoxication of pride and of passions that they deafen their natural fear. Happy those who fearing God, fear him only! Happy those who detached from this life and from the vain esteem of men who are blind, are equally undaunted by the perils of the war and

by all the taunts of unbelievers! They find all things
in God, and fear only the loss of him. Even death,
if it should come, would only serve to crown them.
It would be the end of their dangers, and the beginning of their good fortune. They would no more
blush for Jesus Christ and his Gospel before the
world, than we should blush to be wise among the
incarcerated insane.

So you see, monsieur, chiefly why you should be
faithful now to that so compassionate grace which
you have received. It is to let you see what you
should become, that is to say like a true Christian.
Do not blush for Jesus Christ, and he will not blush
for you before his heavenly Father, at his judgment.
Indeed, we should hide from the eyes of the world all
which it is not necessary to show to it, but it is necessary for it to know that you wish to be a Christian,
that you renounce vice, and that you flee from ungodliness. The real way to spare yourself long argu-
ments and dangerous temptations, is definitely not
to remain on the fence. When a man declares himself clearly for religion, first people whisper, but soon
they keep still, they grow used to letting him go his
way. Bad companions leave and seek other company.

I have thanked God for having given you the Duke
of Beauvilliers during this journey. It must be, monsieur, that God loves you dearly, to be giving you,

after such great unfaithfulness, a so deep desire for
the good, with so much help to sustain you in the
desire. Watch, pray, distrust others and yourself
even more, in order never to lose the fruits of a so
precious mercy. You have been trusted with young
plants which you must guard carefully. You know
by your experience, what is to be feared for persons
starting out in the world, and nothing will be of
more help to them, than to be shown evidences of
your good friendship. Furthermore, monsieur, I only
take the liberty of telling you all this, because you
wished for it, and because my heart urges me to do
so. I should like to see you already overwhelmed
with every sort of blessing. I pray our Lord to safe-
guard your body, and still more your soul. No one
will ever be, monsieur, more devotedly yours.

III

Paris, Oct. 30, 1688

You ought not to think, monsieur, that a person is losing touch with God when he loses the chance to read good books. We owe it to God to profit by so great a resource, when he allows it to us; but when he takes it away by a real necessity he makes up for it by his mercy. Then he himself becomes our book within. He is present in the midst of all the hustle and bustle. He makes the sweetness of his voice heard in the depths of the soul. He makes us feel the vanity, the corruption, and the misery of everything without, and he himself by his Holy Spirit, writes a living and indelible law in our hearts. So content yourself, monsieur, when you can not do otherwise, by saying your breviary attentively without straining yourself. What touches you the most in the words of the Office, will remain in your heart, and you can recall it in places of distraction, where it is not possible either to read or to pray. Then the world can not stop you from feeling how contemptible it is, from lifting your heart to God, for whom alone you are reserving it, from calling on him with confidence in your need, from ruling your words according to his law. There you have, monsieur, an invisible religion which escapes from the world, and which it can not censor. When involuntary distraction has stopped you from having these good thoughts, do not be discouraged. Take them up again quietly. Take your place again under the hand of God and you will be almost as if you had not left it at all. In the beginning, make yourself a kind of rule to lift your heart to God, and to offer yourself to him, at certain hours and on certain important occasions. In that way you will unconsciously acquire the habit of acting in his presence. This will become harmonious and easy.

IV

Paris, June 1, 1689

I can not wait, monsieur, to let you know my joy over the things which you have done me the honor to write me. The two definitions which you cite to me are so right, that there is nothing to add to them. Certainly when a person has laid the foundations of a complete conversion of heart, of an exact penitence, and of a serious meditation on all the truths of Christianity in detail, and their relation to living, many people so accustom themselves little by little to all these truths, that at last they see them simply and steadily, without needing always to begin over again to convince themselves of each one in particular. Then these truths all become united in a certain inclination towards God so pure and so intimate, that one finds all in him. It is no longer the mind which reasons and seeks. It is the will which loves, and which loses itself in the infinite good. But this state is not yours. You must walk for a long time along the way of sinners who are beginning to seek God. Ordinary meditation is your part, only too happy that God deigns to admit you to it! Walk on then, monsieur, in the spirit of faith, like Abraham, without knowing where you are going. Content yourself with your daily bread, and remember that in the desert, the manna which they gathered for more than one day spoiled first. So true it is that the children of God should confine themselves to the order of their present blessings, without wishing to anticipate the designs of Providence for them.

So meditate, since this is the time for you to meditate, on all the mysteries of Jesus Christ, and on all the truths of the Gospel which you have so long ignored and contradicted. When God will have indeed effaced in you the impression of all worldly sayings, and when the mind of Jesus Christ will have left in you no trace of your old prejudices, then you will need to watch for the leading of Grace, and follow it step by step without looking ahead. Meanwhile dwell in peace in the bosom of God, like a little child in the arms of his mother. Be satisfied only to think of your subjects of meditation in a simple and easy way. Give yourself up tranquilly to the truths which touch you, and which you feel feed your heart. Avoid all efforts which stimulate the intellect, and which are much less apt to turn devotion into a pure will, ready to yield itself to God, than into a dangerous vivacity of the imagination. Avoid also all subtle reflections. Limit yourself to easy considerations. Go over them often. Those who pass too quickly from one truth to another feed their curiosity and their restlessness. They even scatter their mind by too many crowding impressions. You should give each truth time to take deep root in your heart, because it is not only a question of knowing. The thing is to love. Nothing causes so much indigestion as to eat a great deal in a hurry. Digest each truth at leisure, if you wish to draw out all its juice and be well nourished by it. But no uneasy dwelling upon yourself. Consider that your prayer will be good only so far as you make it without straining yourself, without getting excited, and without being uneasy.

I know very well that you have plenty of distractions. There is nothing to do but to bear them patiently, and to let them disappear, so that you can stay attentive to your subject each time that you see your imagination wandering. Thus involuntary distractions can not harm you, and the patience with which you bear them, without being discouraged, will advance you further than a more radiant prayer, about which you would feel more self-satisfied. The best way to overcome distractions is not to attack them directly with chagrin, not to be discouraged by their number or their length. I have never seen the book by the Jesuit father, which you speak so well of. I hope that you will show it to me on your return. You know, monsieur, how ever devoted to you I am in our Lord.

V

Paris, Monday, June 6, 1689

I think, monsieur, that the last letter which I had the honor of writing to you has answered all the questions which you have asked me. Now it is only a question of your occupying yourself quietly with the subjects which you have chosen. It is only true that you should make this occupation as simple as possible, and this is the way to do so.

Do not burden yourself with a great number of different thoughts on each subject, but stay long enough with each one for it to give some nourishment to your heart. Little by little you will become accustomed to considering the truths fixedly, and without jumping from one to the other. This concentration on each truth will serve to deepen it still more in your heart. You will acquire the habit of holding yourself to your subjects by inclination and by quiet willingness, while most people only give them a passing thought. This will be the real foundation of all that God may wish to do with you later. He will even redeem in this way the natural activity of the mind, which always would like to discover new things, instead of digging deeper into those which it knows already. It is not necessary, however, to force yourself at first to continue to meditate on a truth, when you find no more juice in it. I simply propose not leaving it until you feel that it has nothing more to furnish you for your nourishment.

As for your emotions, receive all which the meditation on your subject inspire in you, and yield yourself gently to them, but do not make a great effort because straining would exhaust you, heat your brain, indeed use you up; because it would preoccupy you too much with your own impulses, give you a dangerous confidence in your own efforts to stir yourself; and would attach you too much to the pleasure of feeling and thus prepare you for great disappointment in times of dryness. So be satisfied to follow simply and without reflection the warm impulses which God will give you in considering your subject or some other truth.

As for the methods of a higher state, do not think of them at all. There is a time for everything, and the important thing is never to anticipate. It is one of the greatest rules of the spiritual life, to live within the present moment, without looking farther ahead. You know that the Israelites followed the column of smoke or of fire in the desert, without knowing where it was leading them. They could only take the manna for one day. The rest spoiled.

It is not a question of going fast. It is a question

of going well. If one of your servants, on a journey, wanted always to find the way to make the greatest speed, you would say to him, *My friend, you will go fast enough, if you do not loiter, if you follow the route which I shall mark for you, and if you arrive on the day which pleases me.* That is exactly what God says to you, and the way in which he wants you to serve him. Have no other will at all, even for the greatest good, except to follow his. At present only think of laying the foundations of the building, and of digging them well by an entire renunciation of your whole self, and by an abandon without reserve to the commands of God. After that, God will raise on this foundation such an edifice as seems good to him. Give yourself up to him, and close your eyes. How great is this leading of faith, when we go forward like Abraham, without knowing where we are going! What blessings it draws upon us! Then God will be your guide, and he himself will travel with you, as it is said that he travelled with the Israelites, so that he could lead them step by step across the desert, as far as the promised land. How happy you will be, monsieur, if you allow God to take possession of you, to do all that he wishes with you, as he sees fit, and not according to your own inclination!

VI

Paris, June 9, 1689

Nothing, monsieur, should keep you from recollecting yourself in the presence of God, when you are on horse-back and when you can not read in order to choose a particular subject for meditation. But you must observe the following things.

1. Not to let this recollection take the place of your meditation, so that you can do away with it, when you can manage the time to make your meditation before or after your rides.

2. To mix this presence of God with distinct acts and special reflections on the truths which you have already meditated, every time that these acts and these reflections will be apt to renew your feeling and make you more recollected.

3. Never to tire yourself in this recollection, and to relax your mind by little intervals of innocent amusement and gaiety, every time that you feel the need of it.

I feel sure that this presence of God will become unconsciously frequent and familiar to you. As for your way of meditating, it is good, and you have only to continue it, monsieur. Be gay, like a man who has found the true treasure, and who needs nothing more. Live each day for the day itself, without worrying, for, each day, as Jesus Christ said, *will take care of itself.* Thus each day brings its grace and its blessing, with its troubles and temptations. Speak intimately with God. Be simple with him like a little child. The more your will becomes dead to all the vain desires of the age and to degenerate pleasures, the more you will feel a certain innocent and childlike joy, which is infinitely above the magnificent diversions by which the wise of this day try in vain to satisfy their restlessness. O, how sad they are, miserable and consumed by boredom in the midst of spectacles! You will laugh at their folly which passes for wisdom, and you will have the true wisdom, in only wanting God, and in tasting in simplicity the joy of the Holy Spirit. I am sending you, monsieur, the names for the soldier in whose favor I have already bothered you. Without putting yourself to too much trouble, see if you can deliver this poor wretch, and if he deserves deliverance as much as I have been told that he does.

VII

Paris, July 2, 1689

I am grateful to you, monsieur, for the extreme
kindness and the urgent terms with which you have
written to the captain of the soldier, whom they
wanted to try to save. As it was one of my good
friends who wished me to beg you to do this, I could
not refuse him, and I went beyond all rules of discretion in the matter, hoping that you would forgive
me.

Do not hesitate, monsieur, to recollect yourself in
the presence of God, when the desire comes to you,
so long as this desire does not go as far as an over-
long or over-strong concentration. You can practice
this recollection in certain free moments on plenty
of occasions, so long as this does not affect your
regular times of prayer.

I do not think that you should push the rule which
you have made about games of chance to extremes.
It is dangerous to make rules which are not kept. To
accustom servants to obey faithfully, we must only
give orders which we wish them to obey exactly.
Otherwise authority is lessened. For men in livery,
I think we can request them not to play cards, because they play too passionately. The result would

be too great losses, quarrels, and often household thefts, to repair the losses at play. But to soften this severity, I would provide them with draughts, and with other small games proper for their amusement. Therefore they would have no excuse to seek other amusements, but I should not like them to play for money at all. As for the other servants, slightly less honest folk, it seems to me that we need not watch them so closely. You can only talk to them, and make them understand that you do not want people addicted to gambling, who do not know how to keep busy. To keep them employed, you must find the aptitude of each individual. Give something to write to one, small commissions to another, accounts to keep to the next, etc. It is idleness which makes it so difficult to banish gambling. There, monsieur, you have my thoughts on this subject.

As for airs from the Opera, it is for you to know what impressions they can make on you. I say can make because although they might not make them at certain times, they can make them at others, when temptations are awakened. If these tunes should not have any bad effect on you, I should think that you could sing them, but without the words, which are in themselves insipid enough, and which should have no charms for you in the mood in which God is keeping you. There is still another rule to keep, which is never to sing these airs in places where you could be heard by people who will think that your example authorizes them to sing them also, or who will misjudge the sincerity of your piety, seeing you full of profane songs. Except for these things which I have just called your attention to, I hope, monsieur, that you will feel entirely free to enjoy yourself innocently, because joy is very useful and very necessary for your body and for your soul.

The man who makes your accounts can work at them holidays and Sundays but less than on other days, and not at the hours of the Office, which it is good for him to be free to attend. *Cupio te in visceribus Christi Jesu.* This is the wish of St. Paul.

VIII

Paris, Aug. 7, 1689

I have received your last letter, monsieur, with deep joy, because I found great evidence of the goodness with which God is leading you as though by the hand. You were mistaken in hoping that young men gathered together with a man as young as yourself, and one with whom they have been so familiar in the midst of their rioting, would restrain themselves for love of you. That is not to be expected until you become a greatly respected person, by your age, occupation, and character. Until then you must content yourself with putting one of these young men with three or four old officers, so that the boredom and disproportion of the company will serve as a restraint. It is only a mingling which can save you, and it is up to you, monsieur, to do it in a way which will not be too upsetting, and which will nevertheless be adequate to stop the wildness of the young men of the court. You would not be able to put three or four of the same kind together, without running the risk of a great commotion.

As for the past, it is past. You can not bring it back. It is enough to yield it unreservedly to the mercy of God, in order to take to him all the humiliation of this mistake, which is not a voluntary error, and which is only pure lack of foresight. As for your servants, you can only make up for the scandal by your good example, and by your precautions to spare them similar scenes. God has permitted all this to show you by experience what you should avoid. Do not worry over it at all. It is nothing so long as you are very careful in future. The affair having taken place, you could do nothing better than you have done, which is to take it all very seriously, to say nothing, and to end it quietly.

As for the wood which your men burn, this is my advice. I beg you to receive it as simply as I give it, and to have no qualms.

1. I should forage like the others, because you could not do differently from the rest of the army. On a campaign there is no other way to subsist, and you would cause a sort of scandal in seeming to condemn the only way in which the king wishes to and is able to sustain his troops.

2. As for fruit-trees which can feed the peasants, or the wood of their houses, I should not allow these to be burned, nor be taken, whenever something else can be done, because it is only necessity which should authorize such behavior, which, if unnecessary becomes very wrong.

3. As for the trees which are not fruit trees, I

think you should be content to cut the branches rather than cutting the tree, if the branches are enough for your need. Because, as necessity is your only right, you must only do exactly as much, as real necessity forces you to do, and even in this case, one should (not being able to keep from using another's goods) use them with all the moderation and humanity possible, so that you handle another's goods as you would handle your own in such a case of necessity.

4. I think that you should avoid taking from the nearest person in the country, everything which the camp commissary give the means of purchasing in the camp or in the neighborhood, at a price which is not exorbitant. If the price is excessive, and if it is necessary to go many leagues from camp to buy things, these circumstances would make their purchase impractical, and you must not make yourself different and over-scrupulous, by not taking from the nearby country, like the rest of the army, what you could only go to buy farther away with a great deal of trouble and expense. When the difficulty of going to make purchases becomes so great and when the whole army considers it insurmountable, then you can consider foraging a real necessity. It is true that it is an unfortunate thing which is to be regretted, but after all it is an unavoidable evil which

war brings in its train. We should lament the fact before God, but we can not free ourselves from it.

I am delighted to learn that your faithfulness to God increases, although you have no enthuiasm at all or feeling of joy. This utterly dry and utterly barren devotion to God is far more pure. God loves you very much to lead you by this rocky road, where you have to climb without ever looking behind you, but which is the most direct way to reach him. Let yourself enjoy, as simply as a child at the breast, all the sweetness which the divine mercy will shower upon you. For dryness and grace are equally useful, when it is God who gives them. O, how good is everything which comes from him! All things turn to good for those who love God, and whom God loves! May he only reign! To him only be the glory! May his will be done in us and through us, and by spending us! May his will be done on earth as it is in heaven!

Printed in the United Kingdom
by Lightning Source UK Ltd.
120540UK00001B/91